JENIFER HEDRESS

COPYWRITING SECRETS

The Essential Guide for Successful Copywriting, Get a Step-by-Step Guide on How To Be More Influential at Copywriting

Descrierea CIP a Bibliotecii Naționale a României
JENIFER HEDRESS
    COPYWRITING SECRETS. The Essential Guide for
Successful Copywriting, Get a Step-by-Step Guide on How To
Be More Influential at Copywriting / Jenifer Hedress. –
Bucharest: Editura My Ebook, 2020
    ISBN 978-606-983-606-4

JENIFER HEDRESS

COPYWRITING SECRETS

The Essential Guide for Successful Copywriting, Get a Step-by-Step Guide on How To Be More Influential at Copywriting

My Ebook Publishing House
Bucharest, 2020

TABLE OF CONTENTS

INTRODUCTION

Copywriting is an exclusive technique that permits you to promote such things as products, special events, individuals or companies. Copywriting is regarded as one of the most important elements of any marketing strategy.

It should be considered as the tool to help your company promote itself. Your customers or returning clients are familiar with the quality of the products and service that you offer and consistency of your business. However, most of the people find or "discover" your site by the search terms or keywords they enter into search engines.

How is the copywriting performed? Irrespective of the company you have, diversities of products and services you provide, you should be fixed to several important rules. Despite the fact that copywriting has changed during the last decade due to the wide use of the internet, some fundamental rules still apply.

As simple as copywriting might look, it should comprise several vital elements. First, it must have an intriguing and appealing headline that entices your visitor to explore further down the page. It must contain subheadings where main features of the heading are restated. The most significant part of the copywriting copy is definitely the body that tells the major points of your text. It should be easy-to-read, logically structured and coherent.

Ideal copywriting content should highlight the benefits of the product, its uniqueness and clearly state reasons your visitors should buy from you. One should remember that there are plenty of other people, businesses and websites, which might sell identical products and services as you.

In order to be successful, you should stand out from the crowd. This technique should apply in offline and online copywriting alike and if the technique is performed professionally it leads to the increase of the traffic on your website. When writing a sales letter remember that one of the most important elements of the content is persuasion.

One should persuade your visitors to take further actions to make a purchase from you rather than from your competitor's. If the principles of persuasion, action, desire, and motivation are applied in your copywriting, one can be sure that it will bring positive results.

CHAPTER 1

WRITING A SALES LETTER THAT SELLS

Ever heard of the saying that if the heart's in it, the brain will follow? There is need to capture the heart of today's advert weary buyer as a result from flooding sales letters from received advertised products or services.

There is need to follow the required step-by-step structure for your sales letters to achieve results. A structural plan that goes into the heart.

Emotion is the key to buying anything; whether it is paper clips or plain paper, emotions are required to enhance a purchase. Once the emotion is set rolling, facts, specifications, and the likes are used to justify the decision made. Catching your customer's emotion is the main essence of every sentence, phrase and everything about your sales letter.

The promise of gain and the fear of loss are the two emotions that really motivate people. The stronger is the fear of loss. Choosing from using either "How to keep from being sued" or "Save money in legal fees" as headlines will get better a response as an example of a sales letter.

Basic human needs are based on keeping the fear of loss or the promise of gain which give rise to seven emotional hooks. Your sales letter must frankly address as many of these basic needs irrespective of your product or service.

These seven emotional hooks are:

- Free time.
- Self-satisfaction.
- Fun or excitement.
- Popularity.
- Wealth.
- Safety or Security.
- Good looks.

Using all these is more important. So, how do you get them to the heart, or get your prospective customers to act or utilize the copy paradigm? For instance, you will catch the attention if you shout "Peanuts" facing an audience in rows of bleachers in a baseball stadium. Your boss has given you a bag of peanuts that you must completely sell or you'll get fired. Therefore, you must sell.

Use The Verbal "2x4"

An emotional motivator must be used to hit them on the head, meaning you start with an envelope. You can ask "When you saw a plain white envelope, did you remember the last time you rushed to open it?" Remember that you must make use of the promise of gain or fear of loss, written boldly.

Let's consider these two examples:

Gain: In this white envelope, we put a money-making miracle.

Loss: Work hard for the rest of your life and throw this away.

The envelope was eventually open and you saw a boring paragraph about your leadership in the industry having conventional sentences about dedication, innovation, and commitment.

It Goes in a Round File

Making use of our key motivators; the promise of gain or fear of loss. Either must be in the headline, as your reader must not miss it and it must strengthen the headline into watering their appetite to rip open the envelope. Both your headline and sales letter must come together in their emotional impact and the message.

For instance, "You are halfway to getting rich if you finish reading this letter". Our next discussion will be about the body of the copy, getting what to say to leave your existing or prospective customers begging for your product. You must mine the clues to master the perfect sales pitch and get into your customer's emotions.

Testimonial Time

Heard of profiling? You put details of key specifications that build trust in your company and you. This can be done by sharing satisfactory words of testimonials from your satisfied customers. There will be the edge if you can get this from people in the industry that your prospects recognize and you can also make use of photos, phone numbers if you have access to them to boost your credibility.

You can share experiences of how long you have been in the business and share any articles about your company and or its products that were shown in the any type of media. These might cost more as they are revealed from an impartial source.

Having mitigated their fears concerning doing business with an unknown entity, your prospects will be completely sold about your product or service. They won't think about you but about what you can do for them to solve their problem. This is the right time to share your details because you have built trust.

Make Your Customers an Offer They Can't Refuse

Make Your Customers an Offer They Can't Refuse

After your customers go through your sales letter, make them an urgent, compelling and irrefutable offer. Offers that will make them feel they aren't losing anything but their problems. Let's say you combine 3 big offers of irresistible free gifts, terms, and price.

For instance, you can make an additional offer of giving a low-interest rate, for example, a blade-sharpening tool and a discounted retail price for sales of a cordless electric mower. Adding an additional benefit might serve as safety goggles or an extended warranty to raise the perceived value for the electric mower. Your offer is enhanced with convincing benefits.

Use a Guarantee

There is need to take the risk out of the purchase, by giving a strongest guarantee you can, making your offer bulletproof, allowing your reader to know that you are absolutely sure about your product or service. Every customer listens to a little voice that talks in his or her head that "You will regret buying this". Go ahead with this final commitment, back it up with a guarantee.

Encourage Those Delaying

Some readers' mind is willing but the flesh is weak as they want to purchase. They know and are convinced that your product or service can solve their problem. They have been reading your letter and are convinced about your product, it is time to use the emotional motivator which is the fear of loss.

For the example of the mower we are using, you can tap into this fear of your reader because of the good offer on the product, there are only a few mowers remaining or that the offer is reserved only for the next 50 customers that buy or the extended warranty is available only for few days. The promise of gain can as well do the same as the fear of loss. Another example could be to buy now and get a $20 gift card.

Action Call

Use simple action words, keep it simple stupid (KISS). Your readers are flooded with messages every day though they have assurance for your product. Each product has different buying procedure which only you and your staff are aware of for your readers who need it. Stop!

Take them through the purchasing process, either to make a phone call or they need to fill out a form and email it or they need to fill out the form, say so. Let them have the clear ordering of what they are buying.

Always Be Closing

As you sprinkle your call to action all over your letter, ask for the order and follow ABC of Alec Baldwin's admonition in the Glengarry Glen

Ross movie "Always Be Closing". ABC won't come as a surprise when you give another call to action at the end of the letter as it will serve as another reminder or if they are ready to order halfway, they will be notified on what to do.

Use Magical Afterthoughts

Do you think nobody reads Afterthoughts? I bet you're wrong. Afterthoughts or postscripts are the third most read part of the letter after the headline and any picture captions. Afterthoughts must be brief, compelling, drawing on your key motivators of loss and gain, establishing urgency and value. They are places to repeat your irresistible offer to your readers and top wordsmiths use these in their letter.

Use The Order Form to Drive It Home

The little voice behind every customer comes alive again here when it gets to the order form. Some of the best sales are won or lost on the order form. It might come like "Go ahead", "You'll regret this" or "Are you sure of what you are doing now". These can be tagged Remorse of a pre-emptive buyer. Use key motivators one last time (gain and loss); only be brief, urgent and compelling just like previous persuasive arguments as before.

CHAPTER 2

THE POWER OF WORDS
AND THEIR HIDDEN SECRETS

This chapter is very important as to what I'll be sharing. We will have learned codes so that we can all communicate mutually using codes if that were to be our proven best method of communication with our existing or

prospective customers or perhaps learned sign languages if those were very effective.

But I guess our proven communication process is much simpler.

The difference between a salesperson and a telesales person is the ability of a salesperson to meet the prospect physically, gauge the pitch according in a face to face response and through signs displayed by the prospect. Through facial, body language expressions, a professional salesman will immediately know if they're passing a message. These can be noted from the nodding of the head together with a smile and opening eyes in appreciation.

Unlike the salesperson, a telesales person can only appraise their sales from a pitch from the prospect's responses to questioning. The telesales person has lesser work to do, finds the job easier, tries to imagine the facial expression of their prospects while discussing with them. The final conclusion will be from the tone of voice expressed by the two parties.

Prospects have advantages over a direct mail and internet marketer as they cannot be seen nor heard. The only tool for the sales pitches is just their written word. To achieve success in getting a prospect, how written words are passed serves as the solution to successful offline and online marketing.

Irrespective of the form, whether email adverts or sales letter, written words must pass a message straight into the prospect's mind. The only barrier to having your written words get straight to a prospect has to ensure your prospects read your message.

Your "hello", "hey you", "listen up" as an introduction in your headline will determine if someone will read your sales pitch and this ultimately depends on your headline. Your headline has to take hold of the prospect's attention else it becomes a farewell and send-off message.

Ever given attention to a "sub-heading"? Subheadings are incorporated to maintain the interest of the prospect through the copy majorly to the benefit of the prospect to decide to read the whole message. Sub-headings are as cogent as the headline. Let your headline not become a "killer" to your sales message.

How about the body of the copy? Here, you display your talents and skills of copywriting. You have no excuse for using all your knowledge and opportunity of the English Language to better explain and describe in details the features and benefits of your product or service you have on the offer. The English language has all the adjectives needed for your writing, so make use of them as applicable.

In creating a catchy copy, you must remember the word "senses". Using our day to day activities from the sense of seeing, smelling, tasting, touching, and listening. We trust them as they represent the human survival mechanisms, just like other mammals too rely on them.

You can anticipate some types of responses which you can propel into your prospect's heart to achieve maximum contact when you use the sense words alongside emotionally generated words. It is a skill for every offline and online marketer to really understand how to maximize profit capitalizing on words.

Achieving business success is beyond writing an emotionally charged and outstanding sales copy but it is effective to recognize its importance.

The secret power of words must never be underrated.

Entice Your Prospects with an Excellent Sales Copy

The sales of a copy depending on the quantity and quality of the details included whether it is a short copy or long copy. It does not mean more words bring better sales.

There are tips to follow to create a successful sales letter having the accurate structure to keep the reader interested from start to end.

- **Using a commanding headline:** From the start, grab the attention of the reader to make them continue reading. This can also be achieved by putting the main benefits of your product across in a short sentence.

- **Use Sub-headlines to create excitement:** Explain the advantages of your product's features and generate the

27

excitement of your reader in no more than one or two short sentences. Specify the limitations of your offer if you are offering a limited promotion.

- **List the advantages of your product:** Every reader needs to have good reasons to buy your product. Think about what your customer wants and these reasons have nothing to do with your product's features. If you're selling holiday villas, you can put across something like the following...

"Save your money and enjoy the Mediterranean sun on your summer vacations if you want to take advantage of the comfort of a luxury apartment, then you have the most important letter to read".

- **Describe your distinctive selling proposition:** Here, you have to mention your distinctive selling proposition in two or three sentences to specify the benefits that differentiate your product from all the others, then let your reader know you will describe the details later in the sales letter.

- **Establish your credibility:** Credibility is the most important thing to sell on the internet. Before your reader will buy anything from you, they will have to trust you first. Highlight three reasons they should believe you. Reveal that what you say is correct.

- **Describe the benefits and features of your product:**
Describe how your reader's problem will be solved, or how his or her life will be improved. You can be more convincing with the more details you can provide.

- **Give more details regarding your product:** At this stage, you enlighten your reader about everything as regarding your product. Write till you are bored and use as much space as you can.

- **Show your customers' testimonials:** You just need to continue to ascertaining your credibility. Show your customers' testimonials that have already enjoyed your product. Instead of making general comments, mention what your customers like about your product or something similar. You can make reference to at least five testimonials.

- **Get rid of competition:** You can get rid of competition by revealing to your reader the information they need to read that distinguishes your product. Show the elements that make it more preferred to your competitors.

- **Continuously build value:** Continuously let your readers know that your offer is so good by building the value they cannot refuse. A way is to evaluate the value of the offer to the normal value of your product.

- **Outline a summary of all that your customer will receive**: Let your reader have knowledge of everything he or she will be getting from you.

- **Talk about the price of your product:** Talk about the sales price and regular price of your product. Cross out the regular price and let the offer price follow.

- **Highlight your products' bonus:** If you have something extra to offer, share it here. It is also part of adding value to your product. Let them be aware or have a sense of taking a quick step as the bonuses will only be available for short time.

• **Present a strong guarantee:** "Money back" is the strongest guarantee you can offer a guarantee. You have more sales when you offer your reader guarantee for your product at no risk to create a lot of trust and confidence among your reader. With this strategy of guarantee, your number of returns will double up.

• **Lay emphasis on your guarantee:** Eliminate all basics of risk by finishing your sales copy with something close to, for example:

"You are sure the product is for you but you don't have to make up your mind now. Give it a trial and give it a go. If you do not save your money, or does not do all I say or your business does not improve or your life does not improve or you do not love it, let me know and I guarantee you every cent of your money back! You have everything to gain and nothing to lose".

- **Inform them how to order for your product:** Ensure you give detailed directives on how your prospect can get your order placing description.

- **Append your signature:** Ensure the letter is signed using your full name and title.

- **Conclude with a "P.S.":** Highlight the most relevant points of your letter in this part. Your copy must be friendly as much as possible in design and format to allow your reader the time to read your letter. Emphasize the most cogent statements to enable your letter to be read in one or two minutes.

CHAPTER 3

CORRECT COPYWRITING
FOR SEARCH ENGINE OPTIMIZATION (SEO)

The biggest share of the online traffic is coming mainly from the search engines and the two main kinds of stuff which influence your positioning in the various search engines are keywords and links to your site.

Your inbound links show how significant your recognition is, while your keywords allow the search engines to know what to do. How these two are combined establishes your significance and these search engines are mainly pertinent after relevance.

You can get information concerning the way you can add your HTML meta tags to some keyword phrases. These tags serve as street signals which are the way in which they are viewed by search engines; checking your tags, thereafter checking your sales copy.

The outcome from this if both your keywords in the tags and sales copy are not in alignment, then your site won't be catalogued as regarding those key phrases. Search engines also reveal on how frequently a different expression of the keywords is brought into play on your page.

Simply put, you will become visible in the search engine results when a prospective customer searches using those keywords only if you spice up your site with your primary keywords.

It is possible you do not compromise readability and still write a rich keyword sales copy.

How readable your site is, is very important to your visitors. It is the reader that will become your customer buying your service or product eventually, not the search engines.

You will be able to ensure that your sales copy agrees with both the search engines and the visitors by following these guidelines;

- Pages categorization: Before you will write, have a structured plan of the website and try to have your article in the order of those key benefits if you haven't built the website. For instance, segment your categories, for example, "Computers" into different pages for "PCs and Macs", then divide further into Desktops, Notebooks, etc.

With this, you will have the opportunity to integrate precise keyword phrases in the duplicate, by this means, covering a targeted market. Turn out every page along with tagging it alongside its main point or benefit.

- Study your customers in keywords they are searching for: Input the key offerings, benefits and points recognized for each one page, along with researching some words your customers normally use anytime they are searching on search engines. You can subscribe to www.wordtracker.com for around $10 to get updates daily and do understand the result explanation of WordTracker.

- Avoid using single words, use phrases instead: It is worth sharing here but not particular to the duplicate. The main reason being that single words are having excessive opposition. It is not advisable to choose the word "computers" if you are a computer salesperson. You can confirm this on Google by typing the word "computer" for you to understand the reason. Another reason to avoid using single words is that it has been revealed from research that computers are becoming more specific in their search to enable them to become faster in giving answers to what you are searching for.

There is need to ask what's distinctive with reference to your company. Let's say you put up for sale cheap used computers, you can probably use "cheap second-hand computers" as the main keyword expression.

With this, there is a chance of being ranked and being displayed in some other searches. This means that a greater fraction of the visitors to your website will mainly be those looking for used computers. The result from WordTrackers will help to decide the most suitable sentence.

- **Select only the cogent keyword phrases:** For instance, you can use something like "cheap second-hand Macs" for Macs page and "cheap second hand pcs" for PCs page etc. Maintain focus on specific keyword phrases on each page and avoid including keyword phrases on every page.

- **Try to be specific:** Check possibly you can escape using "our low-cost Used PCs" or "our low-cost Used Macs" any time you use "Our computers". Avoid using "our computers". Balance is necessary but if it doesn't have an effect on your readability negatively.

As you know, your site reveals your superiority and it won't be good if your website is difficult to comprehend as people will not be able to infer about it.

- **When using links, include keyword phrases:** It is going to be a brilliant idea when you connect your pages collectively using text links. Don't focus on having keyword phrases on every page. With this, search engines see your site and pages related. It is advisable to have additional text associations if the keyword phrase is a link text. An example will be to include "cheap" below the text link when you have the phrase "low cost used Macs or PCs".

- **Include keyword phrases in your headings:** Headlines play a huge role in the way search engines will place your site, just like the way your customers will check out for your headings.

Search engines and customers view your headings the same way so try to include your major keyword phrases in your headlines. You can include extra headings to help the readability of your site as it will help your customers to scan read.

- **Analyze your keyword phrase density:** Run your copy from start to finish analyzing the density using a density checker to know the initial pass of your copy. You can check this on https://kwfinder.com/, type in your domain and keyword to analyses.

The result will show a percentage for all the important parts of the page to include copy, meta description, title, meta keywords, etc. Higher density is better. Generally, you are good to go if you have at least 3 -5% as result. You might need to run another pass if you have anything lesser than those.

Always remember not to overdo these, carry out the guidelines and you will achieve a useful SEO sales copy. Without expert assistance, it is not easy to balance copy written for customers and copy written for search engines as it could be a little complicated.

You should be able to get an expert SEO copywriter to work on your main keyword phrases at no extra fee if you have performed keyword analysis already. Ensure to utilize the guidelines.

What Is SEO Copywriting?

What Is SEO Copywriting?

My frustrations come from people not understanding about SEO copywriting. It is not the way they paint it and making it difficult to really have a direct target on it. SEO copywriting is more than just about the search engines like the way most conversations, articles, and post are centered on topics such as allowable limits, keyword density, over-optimization. Copywriting is part of SEO copywriting.

The first thing to consider is the targeted audience (prospective customers/visitors) as the promotional copy you're writing is to cause your reader to take an expected action. Your sales copy will be ranked with the elements designed which is the last thing.

The main reason you consider your human visitor first when writing an SEO sales letter is that it will be of no use if your site copy failed to convert your visitors into buyers with all the traffic it will have generated in the world.

Because of these repeating nonsensical talks, SEO copywriting is not getting a good name which is bad for digital and internet marketers. For the site to have shown, it shows the owner wanted to be ranked high for certain main terms.

So, to keep a good name and reputation with search engines when copywriting before it will be too late, here are some guidelines to remember that SEO Copy is unique and purposeful, written for the visitor and natural sounding as it flows.

But first, also remember that SEO Copy is not written exclusively for the search engines in mind, stiff (overly repetitive or forced) and mirrored (altered or adjusted to create new pages by simply key phrases changing).

Some Dos of SEO Copywriting:

You will want to do the following when writing SEO Copy:

- Decide how best to pass that message to your target audience or customers.

- Understand who your target audience is (who you are writing to).

- Construct a plan showing the message you want to pass across.

- Select what the page focus will be.

- Select which key phrases will be incorporated into the copy.

- Slot in key phrases as you are writing so they could run naturally with the needed message, not after you're done writing.

- Ensure those key phrases work well with the planned copy and the page.

- Avoid the following when writing SEO Copywriting when writing SEO Copy. These include:

- Inserting a simply copy page to soothe the search engine.

- Construct a plan based solely on how to have a high ranking.

- Replace "every" instance of a generic term (car) with a key phrase (red, convertible car).

- Shove key phrases in everywhere possible (No, it will sound completely ridiculous but it won't get you banned).

- Depend on useless keyword density ratios and formulas.

Remember, SEO Copywriting is a process of writing copy exclusively for visitors and not for the search engines while including elements to help your visitors and the search engines understand what the page is all about.

You can only be sure to create SEO Copy that is worthy if you regard who truly make or break your site's accomplishment (your customers) and focus on them.

CHAPTER 4

QUESTIONS YOU MUST HAVE
WHEN COPYWRITING

Let's consider someone selling a car. If the appearance of the shop is not passing across a good impression to the customers, no one will buy the cars.

This is the importance of a sales letter despite various means people have included all manners of sales pitches in their sales letter but the result will not be as they wanted or expected. Therefore, you must ensure your sales letter captures the interest of your visitors towards your product after it has been able to answer these five basic questions, which are:

- How will my life be enhanced? It's at this stage you have to understand the emotional pleas that attract your prospects like moths to a flame, possibly they want to become richer, better looking, more popular, or thinner, smarter or they want to save money, effort, or time?

Capitalize on your requirements to attract your customers after you have researched your niche market and you affirm what emotional buttons to push as this will boost your sales immediately. You can confirm this through their nods as they continue reading to the end.

- **What is in it for me?** The number one rule of salesmanship still holds that people will only buy for one reason, which is to get the results from a product (what will they receive out of it?).

You must be quick in catching their attention to achieve this since the starting with your headline. Your headline tells your visitors what they will obtain in one shot through your headline.

- **What will happen if I say no?** There is no telling of your customers 'no', that's basic. Remind them of the problems they are having, the frustrations, how much money they will lose, or how sad their lives are currently, and let them be aware of how they can transform all in one shot, just by a small investment in your product.

- **Why should I trust you?** When it involves them to take out their wallets, in order to buy a certain product, people are incredulous. From your previous customers, you must clear their doubts by giving positive testimonials and stress the benefits of your product.

Explore for forums related to your niche if you do not have testimonials for your product, and offer to give a testimonial for an admiring copy in exchange. You will get a big response in no time, hopefully.

- **Will I be stuck with your product?** You seal the deal here by telling them that you provide a 100% satisfaction guarantee if they order the product now.

From research, 70% of the people who buy a product will not refund it, so, the most important thing is to make them buy unless they have seen something similar before and the rest depends on their choices or they have planned to only "borrow" it from the start.

Not only will you gain an unequal advantage over your competition when you have all these tips to answer your prospects' questions but also let your prospect be informed in your sales letter that you care about their troubles and you have the key that they need.

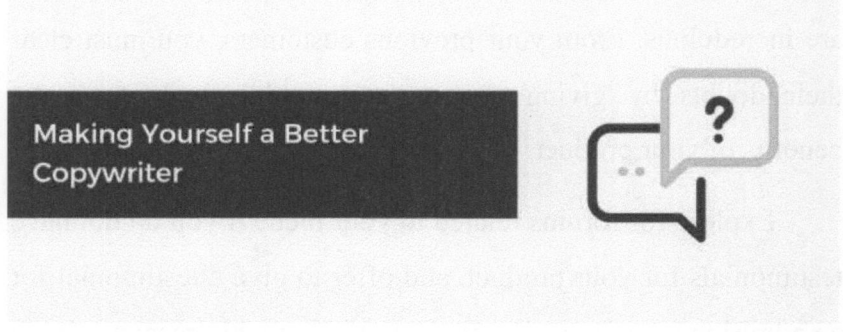

Making Yourself a Better Copywriter

Making Yourself a Better Copywriter

At least most of us are privileged to have some level of formal education on how copywriters use to communicate messages with greater succinctness and force.

You will find these nine guidelines quite practical when writing your next sales web page, brochure, or letter, but avoid being too much of a tutorial:

- **Position the longest item at the end of a series:** When you start with the easy and work toward the complex, it is less confusing and makes a more outstanding ending to the sentence.

- **Avoid the verbs "be" and "is":** Do not write these verbs as they only occupy space and state that something exists. Do write "One simple omission can change from boring to brilliant in a sentence" instead of writing "There is one simple omission that can change from boring to brilliant in a sentence". Likewise, choose that "We will run the fresh program from our office in New York" Instead of "We will be running the fresh program from our office in New York".

- **Specifics are more believable:** Do not use words like several, approximately, many, nearly and other such spongy weasel modifiers unless you have to for legal reasons. Based on tests, research, results, etc. Specifics tell your readers you know what your product is capable of doing.

- **Modify the neighbor:** Make sure your modifiers apply honestly to pertinent clause (Neighboring clause). You'll avoid such gaffes when you do this and as "I crashed into a stationary truck coming the other way (The truck wasn't coming from the other side of the road; it was at a standstill).

You will come across as sober if you had better told the judge that "I was coming from the other side of the road and crashed into a motionless truck". You will still pay the consequence for smashing into a truck, but it is better to tell the judge.

- **Are your sentences like the Energizer Bunny?** You do not have to use serpentine sentences that never seem to end if for the fact that you are giving legal or complex technical information which does not mean. Don't go on and on, for instance, break up and say in a different way, "Laser beams have many characteristics that differentiate them from the normal beam.

They are produced when atoms emit energy in the form of electromagnetic waves", instead of saying "Laser beams, which have many properties that distinguish them from normal brightness, which results from the energy emission in the electromagnetic waves form." See where I'm getting at?

- **Avoid doublespeak, use single verbs:** Distinct verbs can often do the occupation of two comparable verbs. Go for "The computer was running efficiently" instead of "The computer was functioning and running smoothly," Or, go for the straight "He went empty on gas" instead of "He ran out of and was empty on gas,"

- **Show a discrepancy in sentence length:** At the same length, sentences can be boring in a string, so, begin with a short sentence or at least a medium one, and then go medium, long, short, or whichever arrangement is convenient. Robotic occurs if you picture an individual talking in sentences that are all identical length.

- **Avoid overstating the obvious:** Redundancy is not good for clear writing but good for space travel. Phrases like "totally finished", "anticipate in advance," or "vital essentials" communicate very little and drives your readers crazy.

The same is applicable for stringing two or more synonyms jointly like "actions and behavior" or "thoughts and ideas" or just wanted to reinforce one word with a needless synonym or it makes readers wonder if you really meant to say two different things.

- **Go sweet and short:** Why making use of a four- to five-word phrase when a one- to two-word phrase will do nicely without losing its meaning. Words like "since" or "because" can replace statements like "in view of the fact that". This is mainly significant as it is Word economy, especially in a foremost journal, when you're paying for premium advert space.

Follow these simple rules next time you are struggling with that mailer or sales letter, or web page as they will help you to communicate your message more clearly and with greater selling power. Use the twenty- six letters of the English Language alphabet wisely. Always remember that.

CHAPTER 5

SELECTING THE CORRECT COPYWRITING

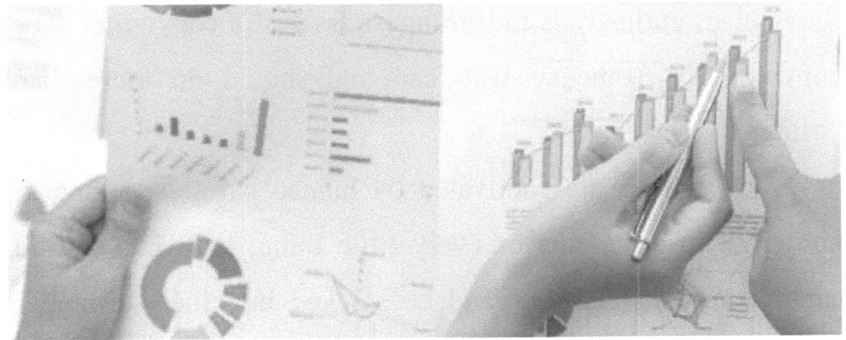

So, how do you affirm you're settling for the best writer since no two copywriters are the same for the job? Choosing your copywriter can be a bit of a lottery unless you know what to look for.

The truth is copywriters range from the not-so-great to the great. Just like any other profession, there are under-achievers, young pretenders, rogue traders, and high flyers. Who's to say they'll gel with you even if you bag a top banana for your project or your product?

You will agree with me that research is the answer. It is better saying no to the first person with a prepared typing finger until you're knowing what you desire by sniffing it out. Remember, curiosity is the strongest asset of a copywriter. The copywriter is someone who can and should do more than writing.

Copywriters are captivated by human nature, wanting to know the ins and outs of every little thing, knowing how to capitalize on inspirations and be stocked into the consumer's head. A good copywriter will look at you critically through your customer's eyes and research your market inside out which is part of their inquisitiveness, not with them being able to play with words that eventually help them see your business in a totally new light.

Curiosity is the key to persuasion whatever your project. This is the first value to look for in a copywriter and persuasion is the only motivation copywriters exist in the first place.

So, your copywriter indicates the curiosity box to show desire as a way with words. But you should discover the one you can spark off and still cut down the field.

When you are weighing up a candidate, try asking yourself a few of these questions:

- Who's doing the talking? Are they listening to you or talking about themselves?

- Can they write passionately? Even the dullest product? About anything? Hire them on the spot if they get you excited about sprocket valves.

- How quickly have they grasped your business? Not just your products, but also your marketplace?

- Your chosen media and industry, have they labored there before? If not, does their other work demonstrate they have a grip on your marketplace?

You'll know you have made the right choice when you have chosen an appropriate copywriter when they start offering feedback. Constructive criticism is sure ways of knowing who professional copywriters are.

They head in the right direction and thrive on constructive criticism.

They will maintain an open mind and pay attention to every point of view but that does not imply they'll roll over and agree to any changes you make.

However, you should see a feedback as a two-way street when you offer it. Great copywriters can realize why your current marketing isn't working and you may have to let go of some of your preconceptions.

They won't dodge from telling you as they will be cruel to be kind.

These small measures should protect you against hiring the wrong person for now. Creativity by its very nature demands that element of uncertainty, there's no guarantee.

You should be pretty close to scooping five numbers plus the bonus ball if hiring a copywriter because it really is a lottery.

Choosing an Influential Copywriter

Choosing an Influential Copywriter

You recognize that a good copywriter can aid both to drive traffic to your website and keep that traffic once it arrives. You already know that professional copywriting is worth its weight in gold.

How to find that copywriter is what you don't distinguish.

It is not something you acquire every week, or even every month, which is the difficulty with copywriting, unlike, say, soda or bathroom cleaner. It can be difficult to know what to look for unlike the products and services you are familiar with or to spot a good thing once you have found it.

Finding a copywriter is simple once you know how, as with most stuff in life, which will be luck.

What are the tips to look for in a copywriting service?

The primary place you will turn to in your investigation for a professional copywriter is a search engine like Google If you're like the greater part of people which is a wise move. As to just what kind of service you can expect, your copywriter's website is most likely the biggest hint of all.

Watch Out for The Following:

Client testimonials: Testimonials are one of the most powerful sales gears any capable copywriter will know that you can use to create copy that converts site visitors into buyers. They're not a good copywriter if they don't know this, then hit that "back" button fast.

You'd expect a professional copywriter to use testimonials on their own site too. Look for a link that states related comments to "customer comments" or "testimonials". Ask yourself why, if it's not there.

Fees: Some copywriters prefer to provide quotes only on inquiry while others affirm their fees up front. Though, make sure you have something to compare them to no matter how your copywriter chooses to make known his/her rates, shop around. Remember, you will not buy the first car or house you come in contact with or lay eyes on.

Neither should you settle for the first copywriter you find as well. Don't make the mistake of assuming that the lowest quote will definitely be the best value once you have some quotes to look at. Avoid companies who sell articles for just a few dollars per time. What to happen is that these companies tend to employ amateur writers, many of whom do not even have a good grapple of English.

Remember, if a quote sounds too good to be true you get what you pay for, it probably is. Ask yourself if you're being quoted considerably less, why?

A portfolio: Without considering some examples of their work, no honest copywriter will expect you to commission them for a project. Spend some time looking at the portfolio on your copywriter's website as a copywriter's collection is his or her calling card. They're going nowhere without it.

How does the copy read? Easy to understand, clear, and not crisp. Immediately you've read it, it should also quicken you to take some kind of action, whether that action is joining a mailing list, making a purchase, or only reading on. They're worth not using if the copywriter's portfolio doesn't persuade you.

Client list or resume: A copywriter needs to begin practicing, there are no particular qualifications. Some copywriters are completely self- taught, having learned their craft from the ground up while others have English or journalism degrees. Ask about their experience instead of requesting about your copywriter's qualifications.

What have they done for those other clients? Who have they worked for in the past? The answers got to these questions will enable you conclude all you need to know about how well-equipped the copywriter is to work on your project.

CHAPTER 6

SUCCESSFUL COPYWRITING NECESSITIES

Content on your website must be appealing, interesting and attractive, irrespective of the product or service you provide in today's rapidly transforming and competitive world.

The role of creating a properly written content copy is what web copywriting will process for you. With the roles of the copywriters to help you compose and structure a copy that must gain the attention of various search engines and enhance your chance of an increase in traffic to your website, those are not enough to achieve success. You must pay attention to how the text will look like on your website.

It is one of the biggest mistakes many copywriters commit both offline and online individuals and companies by creating and writing a sales copy that captures virtually all clients at once. To achieve efficiency, your sales copy must be addressed to each client personally than to a group of people.

It will be a weaker phrase to use "Our services are affordable by our clients" and you will find it stronger if you say "You will find our services are affordable". With this, you pay attention to the peculiarity of your customer communicating and addressing him or her directly. One sure thing is that your business must provide services to numerous numbers of clients; still, you should maintain direct and one-on-one contact with the person. In Web copywriting, knowing this serves as a most useful tool.

Individual communication, simple and direct must be a principle that must be kept whether you are writing for SEO copywriting copies, sales letter, leaflet or just advertisement, if not, your content might lose some resourcefulness.

Ensure you have a simple style, easy-to-read and maintaining person approach when you're writing online copywriting. Your content must be structured to hit a targeted group of audience. It is very important to add copywriting process with marketing research to enable you to know your potential client.

You will be able to design and write content that goes side-by-side with their expectations and wishes. Avoid poorly written contents as these waste skills, energy and time. Avoid it by all means.

Headlines That Will Either Make or Break Your Copywriting

Headlines That Will Either Make or Break Your Copywriting

"INCREASE PROFITS by $1,000s or more by learning one FREE technique in less than two minutes!"

Did that headline not grab your attention? Are you not anxious to learn what this incredible free technique could be?

The reason because of the headline itself!

Just the way you were captured by the heading, so do you have one chance to grab your customer's attention. Your customer can be off by the time he or she gets to the second sentence if your headline does not grab the reader's attention. Immediately, they move to your competitor's offer.

When you have a strong headline, it is unlikely you lose out on a visitor as they will stop to learn more. More sales and profits will be from more people stopping by.

In minutes, you can be making money by writing engaging headlines just by keeping these few points. Overtime when you master this through improvement, you will enjoy the wealth embedded in them awaiting you.

Always Be Specific: Stay clear from the opposition. Use real dollar signs and real numbers as these attract most reader's attention. There are several chances some competition is selling a similar product to your targeted audience. There is need to stay above and ahead of the competitors, specifically letting them know what they have to lose and gain from you upfront.

From the example we used above, we added the increase expected in profits "by $1000s" not just writing that increase profits. Adding this little information, it has added a generic headline to have an attractive offer.

We overlook thousands of messages we come across daily because they create an undisclosed amount of money in an undisclosed timeframe, making it easy to overlook. In the same vein, it is difficult to just overlook a headline which shows how to make $1000 in less than two minutes (This headline drives home fast the idea giving more details and making it a unique technique).

As from today, start to draw customers' curiosity to you with your headlines, leaving the blurred promises that everybody is trying. Make your headlines full of figures and facts.

Make your choice of words: Choose winning (positive) instead of not losing (negative) sentences (language). Headlines must always be positive and stimulating. Let your headline be cheerful, positive, and full of inspiration so that visitors will want to continue reading at the end of every line.

They will be excited and eager to continue reading. Pay attention to the verbs, thinking meticulously how your words will make the heading. How are your actions being currently described? In another manner, can someone portray the same action? Which words are attractive to use?

For instance, you could describe your action of not going to the grocery store and decide to stay at home. This can be done in two ways: "not stepping out to the store today" or "Staying at home to watch the game"

The last quote "Staying at home to watch the game" is more positive for a better headline as it involves positive act (Staying) and a positive outcome (to watch the game). On the other hand, "not going to the grocery store" involves a negative act (not going) with a negative outcome (to the store).

The headline is already bored and negative which will not interest the reader and be sure to have them head elsewhere.

Longer Is Better! Avoid holding back on the critical first sentence, highlight key points, and use a sub-headline where necessary. These are the four main questions your headline must answer.

Remember, we have been taught to be sweet and short in most writing. This could also mean to say few words in as much as possible. This does not apply to headlines. This is only one sentence that must count.

The reader already knows what to benefit, when and how fast they can start benefiting from your product or service. Give more details as much as you can.

- What is your product? (a technique, an e-book etc.)

- How is it used? (effortlessly, directly from the browser)

- Any requirement to using it? (It only requires under two minutes of your time)

- What benefit will I derive from using it? (It doubles your memory; it increases your profits).

Spice up your headlines with capital letters, underlines, italicized and or bolded to make the main idea sink to your readers.

When you have too many important details to share, consider using a sub-heading. Though the headline has captured the whole point, your subheading is to add more information to seal the deal. Avoid making it close together so that it will not get some readers confused.

If your headline cannot capture the reader's attention, it cannot yield sales. The headline makes or breaks sales. Give your headline a rethink if you presume it is doing its job.

It will bring in more success and you will be surprised you took out time to incorporate the main points into your headline.

CHAPTER 7

KNOWING THE CORRECT LENGTH
OF A SALES LETTER

This is one question that always crops up which is regarding the length of a sales letter. It will depend on what you're selling; there is really no one answer to this.

For example, if you are selling a short 20-page report, your sales letter will be shorter than if you are trying to sell a $50,000 sports car! So the best answer is that your copy needs to be as long as necessary to get the buyer to hit the buy button.

For this reason, we often tell people to not worry about the length of your sales letter. Instead, see how long it turns out when you start writing it and you would want to include certain elements and points into your sales piece.

Some Basic Outlines to Follow:

• Headline that asks a question or focuses on a specific problem.

• Introduction: This will be a longer portion where you can tell a story about how you overcame this problem. This is where you address your reader and start focusing on their particular issue.

• Start hinting at a solution.

• Add bullet points about the features of the product.

• Introduce your solution and tell them why it is the perfect choice for them.

- Add any testimonials or reviews if available, this gives them proof that the product works.

- Now introduce the offer: This is where you add the price and statements that say something like; limited time offer, introductory pricing etc.

- Close your letter in the next section and outline the main benefits yet again.

- Add a P.S: This section is where you say something to the effect of; you haven't ordered yet, why not? Reinforce that the product is on a limited pricing structure. This creates a sense of urgency and entices the reader to take action.

Once you have gone through the above stages, you should have all the details you need for your sales page. All that is necessary is to go back and read your copy. Ensure that your letter follows and reads just like a letter.

As you read you should start to create a sense of 'I have to buy this now' in your reader. Don't forget to add images of your products if possible, as this helps them identify with it. This outline gives you the basics of what to add into your sales letter and will determine the final length.

Emphasis Importance On Your Sentences

This is something that all good copywriters do on a regular basis. They focus on creating short sentences that make a statement. If you are accustomed to writing fiction you may be used to adding more fill to each sentence. Adding descriptions to evoke pictures of the characters or scenery for example.

Good copy needs to be short and sweet. These 5Ws are what a good piece must have: Who, Where, What, When, and Why. From these, add facts to these sentences. When these are added, you will be more specific in details you are reinforcing and pass ideas to your readers.

You should start studying by collecting samples of sales pages if you are new to copywriting, especially if you want to make use of bullet points, headings, sentences, and subheadings. Remember, computers and mobile devices will be used to read your sales copy.

Ensure to add texts that are easy to read as some devices have smaller screens to display as much text. Most readers get fed up and stopped reading large, never-ending paragraph of text. Keep it short, and clear sentences.

The purpose of writing the copy is to get in touch and provoke the emotions of the readers to action. One way to do this is to research about their problem and bring it to the surface. Whatever they may be afraid of; fear of losing their job, worried about finances or health, ensure to make your copy address this particular problem.

Showcase your solutions after addressing these fears and this will give your reader hope of a potential solution to the current problem. Be sure they will be buying the solution from you. This requires the practice of your copywriting skill as it sounds simple.

Always remember to write short sentences. Practice more of short and concise sentences. In addition to this, practice on writing short headings and sub-headings. Headlines and subheadings make your copy to be easy to read and make it pleasing to the eye.

CHAPTER 8

THE BASICS OF PERFECT COPYWRITING

Writing good sales letters is a skill that many people should learn, regardless of whether they actually want to be a copywriter or not. If you send a lot of emails, then these same skills and tactics apply to you as well.

The following list is a quick overview of what it takes to write a good sales letter. Understanding your target audience - it is much easier to write to someone when you have a little background on them. You should try and come up with a mental or written image of who your target audience is. What their age is, where they live and their average income, plus their likes and dislikes.

You always want to know the answers to these two questions:

- Why should your customer buy this product and...

- What's in it for them?

Try to find a way to make your sales letter stand out from others: Look for similar sales pages and look for an angle or hook that is different. Have a specific purpose to your sales letter, yes you want customers to buy. But think about helping to solve problems by offering solutions. Take the time to write a good headline. If your headline is weak the customer will most likely not read all the way through on your sales page.

If you are writing emails, then this section pertains to your subject line. Give your reader a good reason to open your email.

Use headings and subheadings: These help to first break up your copy but they also help to highlight the benefits of the product. Remember that 'what's in it for me?' question. Avoid using filler or fluffy words - don't use words such as maybe, hope, wish, try, could and perhaps.

Instead, you want to create concise sentences that are short and contain words such as will and can. Always write your sales letter in the present tense. Instead of saying 'was chosen' use the word 'received'. Using the present tense really helps to add strength to your entire sales copy.

Use testimonials or customer quotes: This really helps to add proof to your copy and if possible try to include a photo of the person. If you can make these people seem real to your potential customers, the better your copy will convert. It also helps to add where the person lives by city or state, always get permission first before adding testimonials.

Once your copy is finished always read it out loud. Either you can do this or have someone else read it for you. When you read your copy if you stumble over a section, go back and edit it.

If someone else reads it see if they are compelled to purchase it, if not, tweak it! By applying these basic concepts to each piece of sales copy you should have no trouble in converting readers into customers.

CONCLUSION

While one of your main goals for any good sales copy is to get sales, a copywriter also needs to have other goals in mind. A good copywriter will understand that they need to build a sense of trust in a reader.

On top of this, the reader has to see the product or company as an authority figure. Once they can identify with it they are more likely to take the final action, which is hitting that buy now button. While the sales copy is viewed as a written advertisement it really is more than that.

A great sales page will engage the reader and make them feel as though this product will fix their problems. That is why it is important to highlight issues and problems at the beginning of your sales copy. It immediately strikes a chord with people; after all, they are ultimately looking for a solution.

Good copywriting needs to be clear and concise. You want to write your sales letter and then go back, edit and clean it up. Look closely at each section and take out words and punctuation that is not necessary. You do not want to add any fluff or filler in your sales copy.

When it comes to following grammatical rules you should get into the habit of not worrying about this. We know that this can be difficult for you to accept. But if you were to follow all the grammatical rules in your copy, your copy will most likely not sell. You want to avoid using wrong spellings and slang, avoid things like pleaz instead of please etc.

When it comes to writing your sales copy you need to get inside your reader's head. Put yourself in the shoes of a potential buyer. Research the product and discover what problems and fears your customer has. What age and gender are they? Once you know who you're writing to as your audience, it will be much easier to write for them.

Another goal should be to have a sales letters that are easy to understand and is hype-free. We are sure that you have read plenty of sales pages which come across as nothing but a major sales pitch.

You want to create sale letters that make your reader feel as though you are talking directly to them. That this product is just the thing they need to fix their problems.

As Einstein puts it, 'If you can't explain it simply, you don't understand it well enough.'

These are great words of advice that every copywriter should heed.

Printed by Libri Plureos GmbH in Hamburg, Germany